Charles Baudelaire, Richard Herne Shepherd

Translations from Charles Baudelaire

Charles Baudelaire, Richard Herne Shepherd

Translations from Charles Baudelaire

ISBN/EAN: 9783744712439

Printed in Europe, USA, Canada, Australia, Japan

Cover: Foto ©Thomas Meinert / pixelio.de

More available books at **www.hansebooks.com**

TRANSLATIONS

FROM

CHARLES BAUDELAIRE

WITH A FEW ORIGINAL POEMS

BY

RICHARD HERNE SHEPHERD

LONDON
PICKERING & Co. 196 PICCADILLY
1879

CONTENTS.

TRANSLATIONS.

From Charles Baudelaire.

	PAGE.
A CARCASS	11
WEEPING AND WANDERING	14
LESBOS	16

From Don Juan Manuel.

COUPLETS	21

MISCELLANEOUS POEMS.

TO THE MUSE	31
SONG, "LET THE VIOLET DIE"	33
THE WILLOW-TREE	35
STANZAS WRITTEN AT BABICOMBE BAY	36
MAY MEMORIES	38
THE BOUNTY OF NATURE	39

MISCELLANEOUS POEMS—*continued.*

	PAGE
NATURE'S FORGIVENESS	40
HOME FROM SEA	41
MEMORY	42
"SLEEP, SISTER, IN THY GRASSY GRAVE"	44
SPRING	46
HOPE	47
TO A PHILANTHROPIST	49
HYACINTHS AND PRIMROSES	52

SONNETS.

"FATHER! I KNOW THY SPIRIT WATCHES OVER"	55
TO W. T. WAITE, WITH A JUVENILE POEM	56
IN MEMORY OF E. M. T.	57
WRITTEN IN DEVON	58
BOOKS AND NATURE	59
TO W. C. C.	60
STEAM	61
FURZE BLOSSOM	62
SIMPLICITY OF LIFE	63
A SAILOR'S WEDDING PARTY	64
TO ———, WITH A TRANSLATION OF THE ODES OF HORACE	65

SONNETS—*continued*.

	PAGE
MAY, 1860	66
FEBRUARY, 1866	67
TO THE REV. S. B. BURRELL	68

ESSEX PASTORALS.

THE ASS IN LION'S SKIN; OR, THE ESSEX CATO	73
CHURCHWARDEN CATO	76
THE PHILOSOPHICAL DOCTOR	80
MY PASTOR AND FRIEND	83
TAP OF WHITECHAPEL	86

ADDITIONAL PIECES:—

PEACE	88
TO FLORENCE AT HASLEMERE, WITH BLAKE'S "SONGS OF INNOCENCE"	89
TO THE SAME, WITH KINGSLEY'S "WATER-BABIES"	90
TO THE SAME, A VALENTINE	92
CANNON STREET	94
PROLOGUE TO COLMAN'S "HEIR AT LAW"	96
PROLOGUE TO "SHE STOOPS TO CONQUER"	98
NOCTES CŒNÆQUE DEÛM	100
ON AN INFANT'S GRAVE	102
TO MY FRIENDS AT VENTNOR	103
TO FLORENCE AT BOURNEMOUTH	105

	PAGE
AT THE ROYAL ACADEMY:	
FRITH AND SMITH	107
COPE, COPE	107
AT RIPLEY, SURREY	108
A VALENTINE OF FORGET-ME-NOTS	109
AT BABICOMBE AGAIN	110
TO ALFRED AND BESSY TEMPLE, ON THEIR MARRIAGE-MORNING	113
ON A DEATH AT HAVANA	115
THE PIPE. FROM THE "FLEURS DU MAL" OF CHARLES BAUDELAIRE	117
A MARTYR. DRAWING BY AN UNKNOWN MASTER. TRANSLATED FROM CHARLES BAUDELAIRE	118

TRANSLATIONS

FROM

CHARLES BAUDELAIRE,

&c.

A CARCASS.

Recall to mind the sight we saw, my soul,
    That soft, sweet summer day:
Upon a bed of flints a carrion foul,
    Just as we turn'd the way,

Its legs erected, wanton-like, in air,
    Burning and sweating pest,
In unconcern'd and cynic sort laid bare
    To view its noisome breast.

The sun lit up the rottenness with gold,
    To bake it well inclined,
And give great Nature back a hundredfold
    All she together join'd.

The sky regarded as the carcass proud
    Oped flower-like to the day;
So strong the odour, on the grass you vow'd
    You thought to faint away.

The flies the putrid belly buzz'd about,
    Whence black battalions throng
Of maggots, like thick liquid flowing out
    The living rags along.

And as a wave they mounted and went down,
    Or darted sparkling wide;
As if the body, by a wild breath blown,
    Lived as it multiplied.

From all this life a music strange there ran,
    Like wind and running burns;
Or like the wheat a winnower in his fan
    With rhythmic movement turns.

The forms wore off, and as a dream grew faint,
    An outline dimly shown,
And which the artist finishes to paint
    From memory alone.

Behind the rocks watch'd us with angry eye
    A bitch disturb'd in theft,
Waiting to take, till we had pass'd her by,
    The morsel she had left.

Yet you will be like that corruption too,
  Like that infection prove—
Star of my eyes, sun of my nature, you,
  My angel and my love!

Queen of the graces, you will even be so,
  When, the last ritual said,
Beneath the grass and the fat flowers you go,
  To mould among the dead.

Then, O my beauty, tell the insatiate worm,
  Who wastes you with his kiss,
I have kept the godlike essence and the form
  Of perishable bliss!

WEEPING AND WANDERING.

Say, Agatha, if at times your spirit turns
Far from the black sea of the city's mud,
To another ocean, where the splendour burns
All blue, and clear, and deep as maidenhood?
Say, Agatha, if your spirit thither turns?

The boundless sea consoles the weary mind!
What demon gave the sea—that chantress hoarse
To the huge organ of the chiding wind—
The function grand to rock us like a nurse?
The boundless ocean soothes the jaded mind!

O car and frigate, bear me far away,
For here our tears moisten the very clay.
Is't true that Agatha's sad heart at times
Says, Far from sorrows, from remorse, from crimes,
Remove me, car, and, frigate, bear away?

O perfumed paradise, how far removed,
Where 'neath a clear sky all is love and joy,
Where all we love is worthy to be loved,
And pleasure drowns the heart, but does not cloy.
O perfumed paradise, so far removed!

But the green paradise of childlike loves,
The walks, the songs, the kisses, and the flowers,
The violins dying behind the hills, the hours
Of evening and the wine-flasks in the groves.
But the green paradise of early loves,

The innocent paradise, full of stolen joys,
Is't farther off than ev'n the Indian main?
Can we recall it with our plaintive cries,
Or give it life, with silvery voice, again,
The innocent paradise, full of furtive joys?

LESBOS.

MOTHER of Latin sports and Greek delights,
  Where kisses languishing or pleasureful,
  Warm as the suns, as the water-melons cool,
Adorn the glorious days and sleepless nights,
Mother of Latin sports and Greek delights,

Lesbos, where kisses are as waterfalls
  That fearless into gulfs unfathom'd leap,
Now run with sobs, now slip with gentle brawls,
  Stormy and secret, manifold and deep;
Lesbos, where kisses are as waterfalls!

LESBOS.

Lesbos, where Phryne Phryne to her draws,
   Where ne'er a sigh did echoless expire,
   As Paphos' equal thee the stars admire,
Nor Venus envies Sappho without cause!
Lesbos, where Phryne Phryne to her draws,

Lesbos, the land of warm and langorous nights,
   Where by their mirrors seeking sterile good,
The girls with hollow eyes, in soft delights,
   Caress the ripe fruits of their womanhood,
Lesbos, the land of warm and langorous nights.

Leave, leave old Plato's austere eye to frown;
   Pardon is thine for kisses' sweet excess,
Queen of the land of amiable renown,
   And for exhaustless subtleties of bliss,
Leave, leave old Plato's austere eye to frown.

Pardon is thine for the eternal pain
   That on the ambitious hearts for ever lies,
Whom far from us the radiant smile could gain,
   Seen dimly on the verge of other skies;
Pardon is thine for the eternal pain!

Which of the gods will dare thy judge to be,
  And to condemn thy brow with labour pale,
  Not having balanced in his golden scale
The flood of tears thy brooks pour'd in the sea?
Which of the gods will dare thy judge to be?

What boot the laws of just and of unjust?
  Great-hearted virgins, honour of the isles,
Lo, your religion also is august,
  And love at hell and heaven together smiles!
What boot the laws of just and of unjust?

For Lesbos chose me out from all my peers,
  To sing the secret of her maids in flower,
  Opening the mystery dark from childhood's hour
Of frantic laughters, mix'd with sombre tears;
For Lesbos chose me out from all my peers.

And since I from Leucate's top survey,
  Like a sentinel with piercing eye and true,
Watching for brig and frigate night and day,
  Whose distant outlines quiver in the blue,
And since I from Leucate's top survey,

To learn if kind and merciful the sea,
   And midst the sobs that make the rock resound,
Brings back some eve to pardoning Lesbos, free
   The worshipp'd corpse of Sappho, who made her bound
To learn if kind and merciful the sea!

Of her the man-like lover-poetess,*
   In her sad pallor more than Venus fair!
   The azure eye yields to that black eye, where
The cloudy circle tells of the distress
Of her the man-like lover-poetess!

Fairer than Venus risen on the world,
   Pouring the treasures of her aspect mild,
The radiance of her fair white youth unfurl'd
   On Ocean old enchanted with his child;
Fairer than Venus risen on the world.

Of Sappho, who, blaspheming, died that day
   When trampling on the rite and sacred creed,
She made her body fair the supreme prey
   Of one whose pride punish'd the impious deed
Of Sappho who, blaspheming, died that day.

    * Et de nimboso saltum Leucate minatur
      Mascula Lesbiacis *Sappho* peritura sagittis.
                Auson. *Idyl.* cccxxv., 24, 25.

And since that time it is that Lesbos moans,
    And, spite the homage which the whole world pays,
Is drunk each night with cries of pain and groans,
    Her desert shores unto the heavens do raise,
And since that time it is that Lesbos moans!

COUPLETS.

FROM THE SPANISH OF DON JUAN MANUEL.*

If any good thou doest, how small soever,
Let it be nobly done—for good deeds live for ever.

Though others injure thee, or spite,
Yet cease not thou to do aright.

So shall a man reach, by a leap, to heaven,
Obeying trustfully the laws that God hath given.

The upright man in all he does prevails;
The wicked in his plans as surely fails.

* Contributed to Dr. James York's translation of *El Conde Lucanor*, 1867.

Who counsels thee to secrecy with friends,
Seeks to entrap thee for his own base ends.

To venture much of thy wealth refuse
On the faith of a man who has naught to lose.

In aim, as well as deed, be pure,
If you would make your glory sure.

He who refuses help when thou hast need
For aid, himself in vain one day may plead.

Who pays thy kindness with ungratefulness,
The more he has to give will give the less.

Waste not your kindness on one
Who heeds not the good you have done.

The true treasure gain,
And the false disdain.

The man is dead and gone ;
No more his name is known.

The man is dead and gone ;
But his name and fame live on.

If for vice and wanton pleasure our good fame we spend,
Life is given in meagre measure, and we miss the end.

Murmur not at God's dealings ; it may be
He seeks thy good in ways thou canst not see.

Do not chastise the erring youth,
But lead him gently to the truth.

By ways and works thou mayest know
Which youths to worthiest men will grow.

The good occasion—use it,
Lest, through delay, thou lose it!

———

God's guidance making thee secure,
Fight on to the end, of victory sure.

———

Hold this for sure, for 'tis a truth well proved,
Honour and slothful ease are wide removed.

———

By the pity of God, and good counsel in need,
A man shall from danger escape, and succeed.

———

In thy chosen life's adventure steadfastly pursue the cause,
Neither moved by critic's censure nor the multitude's applause.

———

Wouldst thou make sure from danger to escape,
Then wait not till it take a threatening shape.

Who risks his life for greed of pelf,
Can hardly hope to enrich himself.

Confine your thoughts to what is real,
And cease to nurse a vain ideal.

Know when to give and when withhold,
Or you may come to want untold.

Let not poverty dismay your mind,
Since others poorer than yourself you find.

Who does thee ill and feigns regret,
Beware of falling in his net.

What avail the eyes that water,
If the hands are bent on slaughter?

If thou have need be not too nice,
Nor wait for friends to ask thee twice.

To lying slanders ne'er attend
Against a tried and proven friend.

Let all thy acts be clear of blame,
That slander breathe not on thy fame.

In quest of this world's fleeting pleasure,
Lose not the more enduring treasure.

The evil man must be withstood,
Till evil be o'ercome with good.

Adhere to truth, from falsehood fly;
For evil follows all who lie.

The ills that touch not life contented bear,
But shun thou those with utmost skill and care.

Be not induced to take a false direction
By promises of safeguard or protection.

Who would not for life be a henpeck'd fool,
Must show from the first that he means to rule.

If your anger hastily you vent,
'Twill be your fate at leisure to repent.

If thou be forced all ways to exchange a blow,
Choose the more distant though more powerful foe.

Mind not the semblance but the deed,
Wouldst thou from evil chance be freed.

Who doth not trust in God repose,
Evil his life and sad its close.

Many things unreasonable seem,
Which, when better known, we learn to esteem.

MISCELLANEOUS POEMS.

TO THE MUSE.

THROUGH five long changing years
   She lit with joy my brow,
Dispersed my sorrowing tears—
   And will she leave me now?

She brought a blessed balm
   When sadness made me bow,
Refresh'd my heart with calm—
   And will she leave me now?

Her torch has lit my way;
   In vain the wind would blow;
She turn'd my night to day—
   And will she leave me now?

TO THE MUSE.

She gave to me the land
   Where milk and honey flow;
She led me by the hand—
   And will she leave me now?

She led to field and wood
   Where myriad flowerets grow;
Her words were wise and good—
   And will she leave me now?

My heart is choked with grief,
   My soul oppress'd with woe,
I seem a wither'd leaf—
   And will she leave me now?

Oh! let her wait awhile
   Till that new day shall glow
When sunny skies shall smile—
   She will not leave me now.

SONG.

Let the violet die,
   Let the primrose fade;
Let the sunny sky
   Deepen into shade.
But—oh! be not so
   'Mid the world's dark roar;
Keep thou true to me
   Ever, evermore.

Let the aspen shake
   Like a trembling boy;
But hearts should not break
   As a brittle toy.
Let not thine do so
   'Mid the world's dark roar;
Keep thou true to me
   Ever, evermore.

SONG.

Let the stream take course
   Downward to the sea,
Losing in that force
   Its identity.
But—oh! stand alone
   'Mid the world's dark roar;
Keep thou true to me
   Ever, evermore.

THE WILLOW-TREE.

Of all the trees that grow on earth
   The weeping willow is my choice:
The oak for strength, the elm for mirth,
The yew to tell of death and birth,
   And lend a warning voice.

But ah! in hours of sober thought,
   When memory views the past with pain,
And thinks on all that time has wrought,
And all the pleasures that though sought
   Will never come again;

How sweet to lie beneath the shade
   The bending willow doth afford,
For lonely contemplation made
When saddening thoughts the heart invade,
   And touch its tenderest chord.

STANZAS

WRITTEN AT BABICOMBE BAY, A FEW DAYS BEFORE LEAVING ENGLAND.

Before I seek another land
    I pause a little while;
Kind Nature takes me by the hand,
    How gentle is her smile!
She leads me to a sunny bay,
    With sloping hills above,
She warms a February day,
    So wonderful her love!

And here I rest, and gaze upon
    My native land's blue sky,
Her homes by these green sloping hills
    Where one might live and die.

As calm a sea, as fair a heaven,
  As summer could have brought,
To compensate for absence given—
  A boon unhoped, unsought!

I soon must leave the sloping hills,
  The happy sunny vales;
The thought my soul with anguish fills,
  My heart within me fails.
Yet consolations will be sent,
  Like those which here I find,
To woo the spirit to content,
  And lift the drooping mind.

6th February, 1861.

MAY MEMORIES.

'Twas sweet, on afternoons in May,
To lie and read in a Devonshire lane;
The blue sky brought me peace as I lay,
My thoughts were the thoughts of chiidhood again.

'Twas sweet in any month of the year,
To stroll to Ongar's pleasant town
By Chigwell's church and village dear;
My thoughts were the thoughts of childhood again.

THE BOUNTY OF NATURE.

Howe'er we change in time or place,
   Kind Nature still is boon and free—
How bounteous and profuse her grace
   To frail mortality:
Bearing the record in her face
   Of genuine liberty.

No feeble lessons she instils,
   No puny morals brings;
Without restraint flow on her rills,
   Her woodland throstle sings—
She shows our weak and wavering wills
   Into the life of things.

NATURE'S FORGIVENESS.

STILL bounteous Nature, though we fail
   In much of what we ought to do,
And though our life be as a tale
   Of things done wrongly which we rue—
Sweet Power of mercy! what avail
   Our lapses? Thou art true.

Kind Spirit! when we lose the track
   By which we ought to go—
Thou still—the star to lead us back—
   Thy radiance clear dost show;
And small the blessing we can lack
   Which thou wilt not bestow.

HOME FROM SEA.

Over the foam did I wander and roam
Thousands of miles from friends and home.
On the rolling brine, sweet sister of mine,
In the roughest storm her gentle form
      Watch'd over and guarded me.
And now return'd from the rolling brine,
Is she gone, is she gone, sweet sister of mine?
      My heart is a troubled, troubled sea.
Sister of mine, sweet sister of mine,
      You are all that is left to me!

MEMORY.

At night's serene and silent hour
   An impulse o'er my spirit bounds,
And Memory comes in all her power,
   Soothing to rest with dulcet sounds.
She whispers stories of the past,
   Of days that never come again;
Of sunny scenes that could not last,
   Of deep but half-forgotten pain.

She haunts the stillness of the eve,
   Borne on the solemn vesper bell,
And sometimes sternly makes me grieve
   For follies that she stores too well.

MEMORY.

And yet from out her archives oft
    Some pleasing recollection brings,
Encircled with a halo soft,
    That hushes all my murmurings.

And thus her power is doubly used
    When she approaches to my side;
And sometimes is my heart accused,
    At others it is justified.
And so she mingles joy and pain,
    And each alternate fills the breast,
Until they blend into one strain,
    And their song lulls me into rest.

Sleep, Sister, in thy grassy grave;
    I did not think that thou wouldst die:
    Around thee shall the soft breeze sigh,
The lark shall chant his early stave.

The ghastly King of Terrors, dear,
    Too soon hath cropp'd thy opening flower;
    Too soon he exercised his power,
And bore thee to thy burial bier.

Thy spirits were erewhile so gay,
    It seem'd not that a mortal dart
    Was nearing ever thy young heart,
And getting closer every day.

Sleep, Sister! oh! sweet Sister, sleep;
    No longer we with thee can talk,
    No longer we with thee can walk;
Our hearts are sicken'd, and we weep.

Oh! Sister, when we both were young,
    We play'd full oft our childish pranks;
    We wander'd by the cowslip banks,
Or daisies in a necklace strung.

Oh! who were merrier than us,
    What happier creatures ever breathed
    Than we, when round our hats we wreathed
In lanes the white convolvulus,

Or roll'd and romp'd upon the grass,
    Or fed the water-birds that sped
    With eager haste for crumbs of bread
We flung to them? But that must pass.

For thou art gone unto a shore,
    A distant and an unknown place;
    And I shall not behold thy face
In all the ages evermore.

1858.

SPRING

Broad trees flinging shadows
  On the greensward fair;
Sunlight on the meadows,
  Fragrance in the air.

Young lambs frisking gaily,
  Sweet birds carolling—
All things ripening daily
  Into jocund spring.

HOPE.

If Hope be seed of which the fruit
   Is scatter'd often to the wind,
And all triumphal noise and bruit
   Be empty vaunting of the mind—
Still, powers that guard the soul from ill,
   O let me nurse the fond deceit—
Of Hope's sweet goblet take my fill,
   Though bitters mingle with the sweet.

For if Despair should pierce my heart,
   And Hope no longer be a guest;
If I should bid him to depart,
   And her to enter in my breast,

Although his light illumed a way
   Through thorns and briars—dreary lands—
It pointed to a happier day,
   A palace gleaming through the sands.

While she with horrid shapes would fright
   The troubled spirit into pain,
And bring the phantoms of the night
   To torture and to vex the brain.
While she no beacon-light displays
   To vary sorrow with a smile—
Though Hope deceive with treacherous rays,
   Sweet guardian powers, let Hope beguile.

TO A PHILANTHROPIST.

'Mid struggling crowds that run the race for wealth,
Few now are found who do their good by stealth,
But gathering up his garments' folds in pride,
The Levite, passing on the other side,
In gilded chariot rolls along the street,
For fear our native dust should soil his feet,
To win the plaudits of the blatant crowd
With sounding brass and tinkling cymbals loud.
Forgetful of her charge, the niggard State
Provides her fostering charities too late;
In ignorance her poorer children grow,
And break the laws they were not taught to know,
Till she, a vengeful Nemesis, steps in
To punish, where she should prevent the sin.
Yet some there are by genuine feeling sway'd,
Who lend a timelier and a wiser aid;
Who, moved by love towards their suffering kind,
Have set themselves to guide the infant mind,

To lift the wretched outcast from the mud,
And check the moral plague-spot in the bud ;
Provide a healthy influence, to cheer
The dawn of childhood and the boy's career.
With wise design, they studiously plan
Through the child's mind to mould the growing man ;
To mend by husbandry the ungenial soil,
And fit them for the allotted life of toil.
Amongst this good and philanthropic few,
The Muse, BERYLLUS, points with pride to you !
By Heaven endow'd with means of doing good,
The world's gay dissipations you withstood ;
And with a modest competence content,
On schemes of bettering the poor intent,
You, out of your abundance, spared the rest,
And earn'd the Saviour's epithet of BLEST.

HYACINTHS AND PRIMROSES.

Such have I seen their charms unfold,
In hues of purple and of gold,
    (A heart-rejoicing sight;)
By me more loved, to me more dear,
Than towering lilies that uprear
    Their heads in vestal white.

Such have I seen in gleaming trains,
In Devon's wild, romantic lanes,
    In such abundant showers,
I deem'd awhile that bounteous Heaven
Nought else for man's support had given,
    But sky, and trees, and flowers.

SONNETS.

PREFIXED TO A SERIES OF SONNETS ON SOME OF THE PRINCIPAL PICTURES IN THE ROYAL ACADEMY, 1858—1863.

FATHER! I know Thy Spirit watches over
My labours—views my pleasures and my pains,
For wandering often through the hedge-wall'd lanes
Or meadows, thick with white and purple clover,
I faintly heard —a wild and careless rover—
In Nature's choral anthems higher strains
Than rise, harmonious, from cathedral fanes.
Sweeter in summer, pipings of the plover,
Sweeter in winter, chirpings of the sparrow;
Far loftier music rolls in murmuring streams.
I communed with Thee thus in my day dreams,
And surely from Thy bow hath sped the arrow.
Look on these humble offshoots— may they be
Not all unworthy of the parent tree!

TO W. T. WAITE,

WITH A JUVENILE POEM.

WAITE, while for loftier efforts I prepare,
Here with the first-fruits unto thee I come,
And bring thee, chosen friend of childhood, some
Slight tribute to thy worth and goodness rare.
Though follow'd close by mirth-oppressing care,
I know thou hast too much courage to succumb;
Grief may oppress thy spirit, but should not numb,
Should rather raise thee to serener air.
Where'er I wander o'er mysterious seas,
Far from the pressure of thy friendly hands,
A gentle thought of thee will sometimes rise,
And years that make us sadder and more wise,
That heal the wounds that nothing else can ease,
Break not the rock on which our friendship stands.

IN MEMORY OF E. M. T.

Dear patient sufferer, thou hast ebb'd away;
Yes, gone at last, after long years of pain
And wasting strength: we shall not see again
That form which years ago did seem so gay.
And no November thine—in life's young May
Thou hast departed; but ah! why complain?
Thou chantest now in heaven a choral strain
Sweeter than any earthly roundelay.
So friends depart, how swiftly! Not long since
My own loved sister was removed from earth;
Dear mourners, then, I sympathise with you,
Who, muffled up in sadness, deeply rue
Her death who now begins a second birth,
Wrapt in His arms who is of peace the Prince.

29th November, 1858.

WRITTEN IN DEVON.

GREEN fields surround me; near are rose-crown'd
    bowers;
Above me there is spread the fair blue sky,
A glorious and celestial canopy
Serenely smiling on the day's bright hours.
How soft and calm the air! Pervading powers
Are present: I their hovering wings feel nigh,
And like a thousand diamonds, lustrously
The sunlit water sparkles on the flowers.
Oh! Nature—mother of emotions true,
Majestic monitress, enchantress bright;
While with enraptured gaze thy charms I view,
I cannot swerve entirely from the right;
Teach me thy lessons wisely how to view,
And thence to gather undisturb'd delight.

BOOKS AND NATURE.

O WELL-LOVED books, in scenes from fields remote,
Ye were my only pleasure; and your still
And silent voices brought me out of ill,
And on my heart a living impulse smote.
But when maternal Nature kindly brought
Her ceaseless riches—valley, wood and dell—
When she return'd—though still I loved you well,
Yet on her charms more fondly did I dote.
Forgive the wandering, but her place is first
Among the principalities and powers,
And when her leaves grow green and her buds burst,
Oh! let me chase with her the light-wing'd hours;
At her delightful streamlets quench my thirst,
And rest within her amaranthine bowers.

TO W. C. C.

Happy the mind that sees in looking back,
Through all the mists of transitory ill,
A bright, progressive influence guiding still—
A certain road, a heaven-illumined track.
The darkest day some crevice or some crack
Will have, to make the clear sun visible ;
And a strong faith, led by an earnest will,
For its support will no incentive lack.
Yes: light will dawn from heaven with rays intense
On him who seeks to lift himself above
The low desires and cravings of the sense,
And raise his mind to lofty dreams of love:—
Deep peace of mind, their natural consequence,
The holy wisdom of his choice shall prove.

STEAM.

Hail to the art that conquers time and space,
And human hands for glorious issues join'd
To carry out the thoughts of mighty mind
That not in sand its characters shall trace.
Hail to the progress of the human race,
Thro' those great men who, dying, leave behind
Rich legacies of thought to all mankind,
With rolling suns and cycles keeping pace.
To work unflinching, to determined ends,
To that which makes our manhood great and true,
Whereon success and high result attends—
To paths which men were guided to pursue;
To that concenter'd mind which never bends,
And dares, in spite of obstacles, to do.

FURZE BLOSSOM.

SILENCE of Nature! when no whisper stirs,
Be mine on moors and hills to feel thy power—
To wander pensive at the sunset hour,
And watch the golden sun, the golden furze.
For if to worldly ways my heart demurs,
If gentle feelings fall in kindly shower,
And Hope enriches with his plenteous dower—
Hers was the influence and the praise be hers.
Her lonely wilds with rapture fill'd my heart,
And brought to me companionship severe
That suited well with sorrow's sullen mood.
No word she spake: her truths she would impart
In sounds to which she forced me to give ear,
In rustling leaves, in roar of torrents rude.

SIMPLICITY OF LIFE.

Hail humble life that seeks no wide domain
To tread the narrow path of godliness,
Which, with contentment, is exceeding gain,
And brings the perfect boon of quietness.
Hence no distracting thoughts the heart depress,
No vain chimeras haunt the healthy brain;
Hence doth the mind, superior to distress,
Unalter'd equability maintain.
Blest is the home, however poor and small,
Where thus sublime simplicity imparts
To meanest acts nobility and truth.
May fleeting years retain unsear'd such hearts,
And on their children promised blessings fall
Who brought them up to fear the Lord in youth.

A SAILOR'S WEDDING PARTY.

BETTER this simple marriage-feast to me
Than sumptuous revels of the vainly gay,
Who, too forgetful of the evil day,
Drown all the fateful hours in thoughtless glee;
But thou, who soon upon the stormy sea
Must seek thy bread and hers (far, far away
From these green slopes and pastoral inland bay)
Where wisest men might learn humility—
Enjoy the present hour of peaceful mirth
With her who sits serenely, link'd to thee,
Yet not without a shade of tender thought;
Happier than those—too high for common earth—
Whose proud refinement is most dearly bought
By loss of nature's sweet simplicity.

TO ———,

WITH A TRANSLATION OF THE ODES OF HORACE.

To thee, the only object of my hope—
(Hope with the world unlink'd) to thee, the dear,
The one bright star that has been able to cheer
My sunless path, as onward still I grope:
Who hast imparted a sublimer scope
To all my aspirations; far or near
Still present with me—unto thee I rear
This toil-won trophy. He with whom I cope,
Giving fresh utterance to his voice long dumb,
Erewhile resounded lovely Lydia's praise;
The music of his strains Time could not numb,
Nor from his brow pluck the perennial bays:
But, fairest, as the votive leaves you thumb,
Yourself be Lydia, and think his my lays.

I.

MAY, 1860.

HEARTS now beat high at Garibaldi's name—
Sicily shall be free; the yoke she bore
So long, despairing, she shall bear no more,
No longer grovel in submission tame.
Then let us to the great deliverer's fame
Lift up our acclamations, bend before
The conqueror with loud songs, nor fail to adore
That Power Supernal whence the victory came.
O would thou wert, thou glory of the world,
From utmost Alps to Adriatic free!
From all thy thrones each purblind despot hurl'd,
Fair land of sun and song,—and then the sea,
Whose white-foam'd waves against thy coasts are curl'd,
Would be fit emblems of thy sons and thee!

II.

FEBRUARY, 1866.

Hearts beat once more at Garibaldi's name,
For Venice cries to her deliverer, " Come,"
The hero watching from his island home
The hour to strike and free her from her shame.
His soul for sacred liberty aflame
Impatient waits the summons of the drum
To set Venetia free, and with acclaim
To chase the mitred Antichrist from Rome.
With deeper and with ever deeper groans
The fair land wept beneath the oppressor's chains,
But now each eye is bright and dried each tear.
Accomplish, then, the hope of Tasso's strains,
The hope that Machiavelli held so dear,
That Dante sang of in prophetic tones.

TO THE REV. S. B. BURRELL.

O FRIEND, self-exiled from thy native land,
For ten long years beneath an Indian sun,
And now return'd, thy faithful labour done,
To feel the grasp of many a friendly hand:
With whisper'd prayers the homeward ship was fann'd
As on she clove her way from zone to zone;
And eagerly was each arrival scann'd
In hopes that it might prove the expected one.
Blest are the seeds beside all waters sown—
And they who sow in tears can well afford
To reap the joyful harvest when 'tis mown
And in full garners for the winter stored—
Loved first for others' sake, now for thy own,
True worker in the vineyard of the Lord.

ESSEX PASTORALS.

[Our friend C. W., whom we all love for his bright, glancing wit, his pluck and kindness of nature, having established a grammar-school at a village on the river Lea, in an edifice worthy almost of some of our great public schools, but not meeting with the full measure of success he deserved, and falling into some temporary embarrassment on account of the difficulties with which he had to contend—an ignorant Irishman who had long been trying to gain notoriety in the village, seized on this critical moment of affairs to write an equally spiteful and silly letter to one of the local newspapers, attacking our friend's system of education, and making a most cruel allusion to his lameness. The letter, which bore the signature of "Cato," was, as we learned afterwards, somewhat curtailed by the editor before insertion. This is the subject of the first Pastoral.

2. Some months later the same gentleman, still burning with a desire to distinguish himself, became one of the candidates for the vacant office of Churchwarden, but was signally unsuccessful, and evinced no small chagrin at his defeat. This forms the subject of the second Pastoral.

These two pieces appeared at the time in the local newspaper, with the signature of "Civis Romanus."

The third piece, now printed for the first time, while bringing the would-be Churchwarden again upon the scene, introduces us to a new person incidentally alluded to in the penultimate stanza of the second — A., Doctor of Philosophy and Schoolmaster, our friend's great rival in the village, whom G., the Irishman, toadied, partly out of spite to our friend, and partly from fellow-feeling. It must be mentioned, in explanation of the last stanza but two, that G. and A. once rode together triumphantly through the village on the parish fire-engine, amid the yells and screams of the street urchins, on a kind of celebration of the establishment of a fire brigade in the village; and that A. had an unfortunate habit of dropping his aspirates, and once gave a pseudo-scientific lecture in the village on the human frame, under the title of "The 'Ouse that we Live in," and was always recommending his pupils " not to 'urry." A confabulation between the said A. and G. forms the subject of the third Piece.

The fourth Pastoral, printed here for the first time, is a paraphrase in verse of a letter our friend received, during the temporary difficulties already alluded to, from the curate of the parish, with reflections thereon.]

THE ASS IN LION'S SKIN; OR, THE ESSEX CATO.

"Causa victrix Diis placuit, sed victa Catoni."

"By Swift, by Machiavel, by Rochefoucault,
   By Fénélon, by Luther, and by Plato;
By Tillotson, and Wesley, and Rousseau,
   Who knew this life was not worth a potato—
'Tis not their fault, nor mine, if this be so—
   For my part, I pretend not to be Cato."
Don Juan, Canto vii., § 4.

Of old, when match'd with fearful odds,
   The hero fail'd his path to clear,
The conqueror's cause did please the gods,
   The conquer'd was to Cato dear.

The new one ill becomes his garb,
   Nor pleads he in his namesake's cause,
But seeks to shoot a venom'd barb
   To gain a little clique's applause.

He arrogates the old Roman name,
    But bears a craven heart within;
And all the forest-kings disclaim
    The ass disguised in lion's skin.

Rather some " smaller beast of prey,"
    Some puny reptile of less span,
Or some gorilla, shall we say,
    That would assume the shape of man.

Can his for Cato's censures pass
    Whose phrases, if not limbs, are lame;
Or lion's clothing screen the ass
    Whose braying shows from whence they came?

O bring your editorial shears
    To make those tell-tale signs more small,
To crop the too-conspicuous ears
    That will protrude in spite of all.

But thou, a silly scribe unpaid,
    Dish up thy catalogue of crimes,
The scandals of each dull old maid,
    With *réchauffés* of last week's *Times;*

And echo back with parrot cry
    The phrases thou hast learnt by rote,
Nor call the thing a plagiary,
    But still misread, mistake, misquote.

THE ASS IN LION'S SKIN.

By what strange error hast thou sipt
    A duck-pond for Parnassus' rill?
Whence came the ink in which you dipt,
    What brother goose supplied the quill?

Fit audience shalt thou find, though few,
    Birds of a feather to thee flock
To learn the code of morals new
    Which thou hast found in *hic, hæc, hoc.*

Within thy native ponds in peace
    Disport thee with the neighbouring fowl;
Web-footed cackler, cease, O cease,
    To make the printer's devil howl.

Ill jesting with edge tools! More just,
    More modest be at least for once,
Nor hide behind that laurell'd bust
    The foolscapp'd temples of a dunce.

Satis ridere. Drop that cloak!
    You wear that toga—what a whim!
It seems indeed too good a joke
    That you should try to pass for him.

CHURCHWARDEN CATO.

WAKING with the early cockcrow, spake he to himself in tropes—
"Now is come the consummation of my fondly-cherish'd hopes.
Bearing in my hands the burden of the apostolic key,
I shall strut it as churchwarden by the pleasant banks of Lea.

"Merit gains the palm at last, and Fortune throws her lucky shoe."
Then the chorus of the fowls repeated, "Cock-a-doodle-do!"
"Fortune," so they seemed to clamour, "lays a golden egg for thee;
"Thou shalt be our new churchwarden, known by all the winding Lea."

Forth he sprang from pleasant slumbers, and he donn'd his gaudiest vest,
Counting o'er and o'er the numbers voting in his interest;
Knowing how the ancient ladies, sitting over their bohea,
Claimed him loudly as the chosen of the village on the Lea!

Briskly on his quest he sallied, and he reach'd the vestry-hall,
Round him his supporters rallied, each obedient to his call;
With a chorus of his touters, "Be unanimous," quoth he,
"O ye independent voters, dwelling by the sylvan Lea.

"Fair are Hertford's modest homesteads, pleasant is the town of Ware,
Classic Edmonton is charming, Stratford's spire is wondrous fair;
But, although their size be greater, what are they compared with thee,
My adopted village, Leyton, gem of all the wandering Lea!

"From the land of the potato, here I came and fix'd my tent,
Here I courted fame as Cato, little dreaming what it meant ;
Here I lately raised a clamour, and the censor tried to be
Of the morals and the grammar of the youth who dwell on Lea!

"Here at last I gain the summit of my fondly-cherish'd hope,
'Twixt the parson and the beadle Fate has fix'd my horoscope."
But his incoherent maundering fail'd to gain ev'n two or three,
And his weary hearers wish'd him—at the bottom of the Lea.

He began to fume and fidget at the absence of applause,
Seeing not a single digit lifted to support his cause.
"Hands are counted by the hundred, not a hand is raised for me ;
O for a warning voice that thunder'd, 'Woe to the inhabitants on Lea!'

"I will rise and quit this thraldom ere the dog-days seal my fate;
Shall I kiss the feet of A——, and attack the legs of W——?
'Tis myself that in a jiffey will recross the Irish Sea,
Are not Shannon and the Liffey better than the stream of Lea?"

Home he walk'd with footsteps laggard, on the ground his eyes he bent,
Took a pinch of Irish Blackguard to appease his discontent.
Pacing round and round his garden ever groans and mutters he,
"Walks another as churchwarden by the hated shores of Lea!"

THE PHILOSOPHICAL DOCTOR.

To a village remote from the noise of the town,
A pedagogue came with his ferule and gown,
" And the better to blow my own trumpet," said he
" I will startle their wits with a foreign degree.

" 'Tis a neat little title : they'll swallow the bait ;
In the absence of silver, why not German plate ?
In these Brummagem times of so much that is spurious,
Are the villagers likely to prove over-curious ?"

So, swoln with bought honours, he Doctor'd himself
In the hope that all rivals might thus get the shelf ;
But one said, " Not too fast, O my brave salamander,
What is sauce for the goose is sauce, too, for the gander !"

THE PHILOSOPHICAL DOCTOR.

Philosophical Doctor by Germany dubb'd,
When he found his pretensions began to be snubb'd,
He could only declaim with an impotent stammer
'Gainst this newfangled 'ellish invention of grammar.

Through a zealous ally, who claimed Roman descent,
He demanded indignantly what it all meant ;
Though some whisper'd his friend had ne'er tasted Falernian,
Through his thin mask detecting a rowdy Hibernian.

As these birds of a feather met after defeat,
One bright morning of May, in the sweltering street,
His discomfited champion the Doctor caress'd,
And in these measured words the great Cato address'd :—

" Remember the day when the crowd did admire
As we rode, like Elias, on a chariot of fire,
Or while ever my audience would dwindle to fewer,
I lectured on second-hand science from Brewer !

"Then wherefore despond, O illustrious Roman?
Stand forth, nothing daunted, my champion and showman.
Continue to mangle, while venting your spleen,
The tongue of our Sovereign Lady the Queen,

"Till freed from this turmoil, and tumult, and worry,
We shall cease to do aught 'neath the influence of 'urry;
Till the 'ouse that we live in its frail tenant yields,
And I wander with thee in Elysian fields."

MY PASTOR AND FRIEND.

" By my clerical coat, by my surplice and band,
No longer my name as your patron shall stand,
But though my protection no longer I lend,
I still shall remain—your Pastor and Friend.

" An unfortunate man I can never assist,
My name must at once be erased from your list;
But this need not prevent you at church to attend,
Every Sunday, the words of your Pastor and Friend.

" I have heard all the stories they tell in the town—
Mrs. Jones, Mrs. Smith, and my friend Mrs Brown;
To their tea-table tattle my ears I must lend,
Or much influence be lost to your Pastor and
    Friend."

I shed a few tears, but my eyes soon did wipe,
And I said, as I lit with the letter my pipe,
"Cast not pearls before swine, lest they turn back and rend,
Nor your twaddle before me, my reverend friend!

"Cast out from thine own eyes" (you know what I quote)
"The beam, ere thou find in thy brother's the mote;
From my foes I am ready myself to defend,
But save me, O Heaven, from a fair-weather friend!

"A Pastor! a shepherd to watch o'er the sheep,
From danger to guard, and from injury keep;
The limping and weak to protect and to tend;
Is not this the ideal of a Pastor, my friend?

"But if he should spurn from him those that are sick,
And comfort the wounded with naught but a kick,
All his care on the healthy and fat ones should spend,
And yet call himself smoothly a Pastor and Friend?

"In the twilight of Time, amidst error and pride,
With little to comfort us long at our side,
What heavenlier boon can the Destinies send
Than a faithful and tried and long-suffering Friend?

"But you and your pastorals—faugh! we've enough—
We care not for—laugh at—the cant and the stuff;
You may drivel and snivel away to the end;
You may go to the devil, my Pastor and Friend."

TAP OF WHITECHAPEL.

Tap of Whitechapel! whenever I think
Of the time when I pass'd thee and never did drink,
The thought to this day will my memory vex
That I quaff'd no libations to thee, Double X!

For how often our lips to the tankard we press'd
To which thirst and fatigue ever added a zest,
And we went on our way and were serious or laugh'd,
Refresh'd by the wholesome and generous draught.

We talk'd of the past and its memories sad,
Of the future that all in gay colours was clad,
Of the outcasts who fester in alley and slum,
And the ages of purification to come.

Tap of Whitechapel! if I could recall
Those earlier days I would suffer them all,
Would pass once again thro' the fire for the truth,
The faith and the hope and religion of youth.

We must drink of the cup whether bitter or sweet,
And the years fly away upon fugitive feet,
And they leave me to nurse unavailing regret
That cannot be drown'd in the best heavy-wet.

Yet if thou hast led to a haven at last,
And I can unite the to-come with the past,
I might find me a harbour from sorrow and pain,
And rise like the bird from my ashes again!

PEACE.

To those who hope for no return
   To honour's lost or yielded place,
How kind and merciful the urn
   That covers ruin and disgrace.

The steps that trod in error's way
   Are seen, for good or ill, no more;
The foolish heart that went astray
   Now learns and loves a different lore.

For with the dead is peace at last,
   The power of slight and malice cease,
The bivouac o'er, the conflict past,
   They rest in their perpetual peace.

TO FLORENCE AT HASLEMERE,

WITH BLAKE'S "SONGS OF INNOCENCE."

Accept, dear child, these songs of one whose Muse
For happy children piped her sweetest lays,
Nor deem'd their suffrages her lightest praise
Who hold Heaven's kingdom as their proper dues.
And wilt thou with the lyric gift refuse
His thanks, whose drooping spirits thou couldst raise
By airy gestures, graceful as a fay's
Dancing at eve in shady avenues?

   With rapt delight I see you ponder long
The gentle words of one so pure of blame,
Who loved the right, who scorn'd and loathed the wrong—
O future heiress of his double fame,
Whose smile, whose look, nay, even whose very name
Recalls the sunny land of art and song.

August 20, 1869.

TO THE SAME.

WITH KINGSLEY'S "WATER-BABIES."

HERE is the promised story; tho'
   You who so sweetly laugh and rail,
What can a fairy such as you
   Want with a fairy tale?

But now, while April's pleasant days
   Alternate rain and sunshine bring,
And everything on earth obeys
   The spirit of the spring—

For now the sky is soft and gay,
   Amid the leaves the sunbeams dance,
All life seems one long holiday,
   And all things breathe romance—

"WATER-BABIES."

Fair weather on your path befall,
 All angels guard with special care,
Who, like the sun that shines for all,
 Have sweetness, and to spare.

And while you con with eager look
 A tale that mingles gay with grave,
Receive all influence from the book
 Of gentle thoughts and brave.

April, 1870.

TO THE SAME.

A VALENTINE.

My sweet little playmate, whose silvery voice
Makes my heart, when 'tis saddest, rebound and
    rejoice;
Whose innocent laughter and childish replies
Are more to my soul than the words of the wise;

As you trip like a fairy the pathways along
Each footfall to me is melodious with song;
Each look and each tone in my spirit gives birth
To thoughts too divine for this grovelling earth.

How vain and how fruitless the effort of years,
How we wander and squander our hopes and our
    fears!
Over sea, over land, without rest did I roam,
Yet found what was dearest and sweetest at home.

A VALENTINE.

May he who once bade little children come near,
And who numbers each thread of that beautiful hair,
Still guide you along the bright course of your teens,
And lead you thro' fairest and loveliest scenes.

February 14, 1871.

ST. SWITHIN'S, CANNON STREET.

MARCH 24, 1870.

MIDST the noise and the roar betwixt Paul's and the river,
Where the full tide of life flows for ever and ever,
Is a gloomy old church that the passers scarce see,
But its weather-stain'd front is delightful to me.

Ere the bitter bleak March could to April give way,
I felt in my spirit the radiance of May;
With the voices of spring did my spirit keep tune,
With the sweetness of summer, the splendour of June.

'Twixt the stately emporiums the broadway extends,
Where we pass'd in old days on our rambles with friends,
Little weeting what soon would make sacred the spot,
And live in our memory when these were forgot.

And now, when I walk through its murk and its mud,
The hopes of the future will blossom and bud;
It loses its aspect of fog and of dun,
And shines in a light of ineffable sun.

Its dingy surroundings are nothing to me;
They are lost in a dream I am dreaming of thee;
Its gloomy old church, and its chimneys and shops,
Have more of romance than a summer-lit copse.

So, from common materials, the great human heart
Of itself can make all things, the vilest, a part;
Mix the bad with the good, blend the new with the old,
And by wonderful alchemy change them to gold.

PROLOGUE

TO COLMAN'S COMEDY OF THE "HEIR AT LAW," PLAYED BY THE SCHOLARS OF ST. JOHN'S COLLEGE, ANERLEY, DECEMBER 15, 1869.

To-night no practised actors tread the stage
To lash the follies of the present age,
No Roscius all the world of fashion draws
To greet his name with peals of loud applause;
No veteran comes with quirk and happy hit
To move the cachinnations of the pit,
With knowing winks and with suggestive nods,
Draw down re-echoing thunder from the gods;
No mighty genius ere the curtain falls
Thaws even the icy calmness of the stalls.
Untried beginners in the histrio's art,
With painful effort each has conn'd his part;
Judged by too high a standard we might fail,
Before an audience more severe might quail.

PROLOGUE, 1869.

No doleful tragedy we bring to-night
To move your pity or your tears excite;
The humours of a former time we show,
What pleased your grandsires seventy years ago.
And if our author's wit your smiles assist,
We still may hope your favour to enlist,
May crave from judgment harsh to be exempt,
And bid you smile upon our first attempt.

PROLOGUE

TO GOLDSMITH'S COMEDY "SHE STOOPS TO CONQUER," PERFORMED BY THE SCHOLARS OF ST. JOHN'S COLLEGE, ANERLEY, DECEMBER 14, 1870.

WITH anxious hopes not quite unmix'd with fear,
Our youthful actors once again appear,
And leaving graver studies for awhile,
They seek to win you to a kindly smile.

Yet here we need not for our author plead:
Enroll'd a century with the illustrious dead,
His humour stands the searching test of time,
As fresh to-day as in its earliest prime.
And like good wine long kept that needs no bush,
We feel it cannot put us to the blush
Could we succeed to catch to-night, as erst,
Aught of the skill of those who play'd it first,

Or those great actors in succeeding years,
Whose sallies waken'd mirth, whose pathos tears ;
Not ours the grace, the brilliance is not ours
That made the house forget the passing hours ;
Not ours the supple movement, the quick ease—
Our only claim, anxiety to please.

 With fluttering hearts, and hopes and fears combined,
Our youthful actors now await behind ;
Yet ere the curtain rise upon their parts,
Let me appeal one moment to your hearts.
If here and there a bashful actor halt,
We pray you gently overlook the fault,
Nor let the bad delivery mar the jest,—
" In mercy spare us if we do our best."

NOCTES CŒNÆQUE DEÛM.

To W. T. W.

WHAT you think, dear old friend, of deserting our Club,
Which you were the first to create and to dub?
It cannot be true! but, however you laugh,
I will write prematurely this brief epitaph.

Prematurely, I said, for on reaching two score,
I might mutter or murmur just this, nothing more—
'Tis a habit I have as I wander along,
And some dozen years hence I might break into song :—

" He left us in umbrage and sought other climes,
But perhaps he may now and then think of old times:
Perhaps as his wearisome journey he plods,
He remembers the suppers and nights of the gods,

"When the wit was as rare as the foaming champagne,
When the care and despair of our life all seem'd vain,
And lightly from mouth unto mouth pass'd the jest,
The merry *bon mot*,—and still his was the best.

"When our talk was so various, and ever we prosed
(With a whiff or a draught of LL interposed)
Of physic, of law, of affairs of the heart,
And of moribund dynasties soon to depart.

"Nor beauty was wanting to grace the gay throng,
And heighten our pleasure with dance and with song,
And creatures of heavenly feature and mould
Made earth seem awhile like the Eden of old.

"He may have gone farther and fared but the worse;
His eyes may ne'er light on my dolorous verse;
But we miss him among us, and would he were here
To heighten the wit and to join in the cheer."

April 10*th*, 1871.

ON AN INFANT'S GRAVE IN NORWOOD CEMETERY.

Now, while the fervid summer is full of glory and sweetness,
  This is our consolation as we lay thee in the sod,
That we leave thy little life in all its incompleteness
  To receive its consummation in the bosom of our God,
Who lighteth up the darkness when our faith and hope grow dim,
And who bids the little children to approach and come to him.

1870.

TO MY FRIENDS AT VENTNOR.

With the myriad tones of the many-voiced sea,
What need of an epithalamium from me,
Or what can I write that avails you to read?
For more gracious than song is the life that you lead.

Yet I call for the Muse, and she favours at last,
And shows me kaleidoscope views of the past;
The palatial dwellings of sombre Madrid,
In the sunny and beautiful land of the Cid,

Where a childish existence is passing away,
In picturesque places of sport and of play,
And yours in an atmosphere murky and dun,
Till two separate lives shall be blended in one.

Your life that so bravely was fought against odds
(And who serveth himself shall be served by the
    gods),
That never would swerve from the sober and solid,
Yet only by fools would be counted as stolid.

The witty and brilliant were little or nought,
For life is an action, and is not a thought;
And even the stars, in their infinite beauty,
Are obeying fix'd laws and fulfilling their duty.

O mystery of Fate! what polarity sweet
Ordain'd from of old that your lives should thus meet?
O force of Free Will! that when once you drew near
Made each to the other most dear of the dear!

I watch'd you with pleasure from June unto June,
Two hearts that for ever were beating in tune,
From the fall to the winter, and on thro' the spring,
Till the day when he gave you the mystical ring.

At the altar I stood as you plighted your troth,
And fervently pray'd for a blessing on both;
That Love might continue to hold his soft sway,
And the longest prove also the happiest day!

June 21, 1871.

TO FLORENCE AT BOURNEMOUTH.

AUGUST 20, 1871.

With the sound of the summer and scent of the pines,
What sweetness is left in my faltering lines?
When millions of bees make continual hum
Perhaps it were better that I should be dumb.

But or ever fierce August give way to the fall
I must speak my full heart, or must speak not at all,
Must blend my poor song with the music and mirth
That give joy to the heavens, that gave you to the earth.

For how often the past and the future would vex,
And the secret of life, still unsolved, would perplex,
Till I look'd on a face with no wrinkle of care,
And gratefully found it interpreted there.

TO FLORENCE AT BOURNEMOUTH.

Had I Tizian's pencil, Petrarca's soft tongue,
How nobly you then should be painted and sung;
Till the end of the world should each gesture and look
Shine out on my canvas, or live in my book.

For ever the eyes should be brilliant as now,
For ever the loose and long tresses should flow,
The glow of the colours, the ring of the rhyme,
Should defy all the subtle encroachments of time.

The world might grow old, and our hearts might grow cold,
Absorb'd in the struggle for fame and for gold,
But you should be there, with the loose flowing hair,
And the sly searching eyes and the innocent air.

Live, happy and bright, in your youth and your grace,
Shedding sunshine around what were else commonplace,
Making flowers to spring up on the sward as you dance,
And filling the air that you breathe with romance.

AT THE ROYAL ACADEMY.

MAY, 1871.

The Gambling Hall at Homburg.   FRITH.
The Last Scene at a Gambler's House.   SMITH.

FRITH and Smith, Smith and Frith,
You are kith and kin, you are kin and kith.
Is there more of sap or pith
In Smith or Frith, in Frith or Smith?

AT THE ROYAL ACADEMY.

MAY, 1872.

COPE, Cope, how can we hope
In work of yours to find any scope,
Though, with many a flowery trope,
Newspapers give you the softest of soap?

AT RIPLEY, SURREY.

TALL lily blooming here in grace
 In Heaven's own blest sunshine,
The smiling splendours of thy face
 Were but a moment mine.

Transplanted from thy garden-ways
 Thou soon wouldst droop and pine,
Bloom thou within thy proper place,
 And let me fade in mine.

September 1872.

A VALENTINE OF FORGET-ME-NOTS.

To F. L. C.

Playmate of happier days and brighter hours,
    The tutelary saint who guards this day
And makes it bright, in spite of gloom and showers,
    With sunshine of the heart, that never fades away—
    Bids me some token at your feet to lay
Of unforgotten summers that were ours ;
    What fitter than these children of the May
For one who took her name from the sweet flowers ?
I breathe a prayer unto the powers divine
    In whose regard is childhood hallow'd most,
To guide your footsteps on to womanhood
With all rich influences pure and good,
That in your growing beauty and grace may shine
    Her gentle spirit whom we loved and lost.

February 14*th* 1873.

AT BABICOMBE AGAIN.

No common feelings move the mind
    As here I gaze again
On beauteous scenes once left behind
    With deep and heartfelt pain.
They woke a song in days of yore,
They well may wake a song once more.

As if to mock the lapse of years
    Past as a tale that's told;
As if to chide the foolish tears
    That down my cheeks have roll'd,
The sky, the hills, the sunny bay,
Are lovely as of old to-day.

Although but yester-morn the world
    Was wrapt as in a shroud,
While, to the ancient city whirl'd,
    We join'd the busy crowd.
The hills above, the fields below,
Were cover'd with crystalline snow.

AT BABICOMBE AGAIN.

I mark'd the rapid river foam
   And haste to the sea to flow,
The little town across, the home
   Of fourteen years ago.
I pass'd into the minster glooms,
The silence of the knightly tombs.

That ghost-like covering disappears,
   The sun ablaze with gold,
The bay its former beauty wears,
   For Nature grows not old ;
She warms with unaccustom'd ray
Another February day.

'Tis hush'd and calm as a smooth lake,
   That belt of sea below ;
I watch its glassy surface take
   Cloud-tint and sunny glow—
The noiseless course of outbound skiffs,
The luminous line of distant cliffs.

Along the roadside, golden-gay,
   The furze is fired with bloom,
And here and there the children play,
   Blind to the coming doom.
With unavailing sighs and tears
I muse upon the vanish'd years,—

The gulf of years that separate
   The present from the past,
And all the havock wrought by fate,
   Since here I loiter'd last :
The sad sweet memories of yore,
The dear ones who are gone before.

My thoughts are of a sombre hue,—
   Not like that soft bright sky,
Light-blue against the sea's dark-blue—
   But of far different dye ;
Yet haply for such thoughts to rise
Is fitting Lenten exercise.

But see ! the golden sun intense
   Has borrow'd rays from June,
And his resistless influence
   Compels a blither tune ;
Chanting aloud from slope to slope
Of resurrection and of hope.

February 26*th* (*Ash Wednesday*), 1873.

TO ALFRED AND BESSY TEMPLE, ON THEIR MARRIAGE-MORNING.

On this day of all days to you can I refrain
From greeting you, kinsman, in jubilant strain,
From invoking a blessing from Heaven on your life,
And on that of your beautiful newly-made wife?

For a century past, in the far 'auld lang syne,'
Your forefathers' fate had been blended with mine;
God grant the tradition our grandsires begun
May long be transmitted from sire unto son!

O true hearts and brave, link'd together so long,
I bring you my tribute of jubilant song,
In the beautiful time of the new-budding spring,
The bright resurrection of everything,—

The season that wakes the desire that lay dead,
And when fair hope succeeds to the long nights of dread,
When the new light is sweet on the woods and the ways,
The season of promise and lengthening days.

Bread of love, on the waters so long ago cast,
And crown'd with its lawful fruition at last,
' For richer, for poorer, for better, for worse,'
O love, that does shame to our stammering verse!

O true hearts and brave, strong in youth and in truth,
Let the future then bring you its joy or its ruth,
Ye slowly by gradual effort shall climb
To a life more poetic than all things in rhyme.

May they fall on you lightly, the fair April showers,
May you have your full time of the roses and flowers,
May your loves intertwine like the myrtle and vine,
And prove the auspicious forerunners of mine!

March 1876.

ON A DEATH AT HAVANA.

MAY 7, 1877.

The leaves are green upon the trees,
There is a gladness in the breeze;
The tired heart feels unwonted ease
  This summer morning.

The lilac and laburnum glow,
The chesnuts stand in lordly row,
The apple-blossoms rain their snow,
  The earth adorning.

When lo! what news is this I hear,
What sudden shock breaks on my ear,
That blots the sun, the leaves makes sere,
  Turns all to mourning?

And art thou gone so soon to rest,
Of all our loves the loveliest,
There in thy far home in the West,
  So soon departed?—

ON A DEATH AT HAVANA.

You left our darken'd hemisphere
With gloomy winter in your rear,
And now from both you disappear,
  And, broken-hearted,

We think of one so fair and good
In the full years of April blood,
Death's fateful arrow unwithstood
  Pass'd from our vision.

Shine forth, clear star, from out the West,
From that bright region of thy rest
On those who loved thee first and best,
  From realms Elysian!

THE PIPE.

(*From the "Fleurs du Mal" of Charles Baudelaire.*)

A POET's pipe am I;
   And my Abyssinian tint
   Is an unmistakable hint
That he lays me not often by.

When he is with grief o'erworn,
   I smoke like the cottage where
   They are cooking the evening fare
For the labourer's return.

I enfold and cradle his soul
In the vapour moving and blue
That mounts from my fiery mouth;

And there is power in my bowl
To charm his spirit and soothe,
And heal his weariness too.

A MARTYR.

DRAWING BY AN UNKNOWN MASTER.

(*From Charles Baudelaire.*)

AMIDST the broider'd stuffs, the flagons deep
    And sumptuous fittings old,
Marbles and pictures, perfumed robes that sweep
    In many an idle fold,

In a close room which, like a greenhouse, has
    A poisonous air and stale,
Where dying nosegays coffin'd up in glass
    Their final sigh exhale,

A headless corpse the satiate pillow-stains,
    Pouring in rapid flood,
Which the cloth drinks, as thirsty fields the rains,
    A red and living blood.

Like ghostly visions that at dusk appear,
    Which hold the spell-bound sight,
The head, with all its mass of rich dark hair,
    And wealth of jewels bright,

The dreamless head, even as a pluck'd red flower,
   On the bed-table lies;
A vague blank look, as of the twilight hour
   Escapes the sunken eyes.

Upon the bed the naked trunk displays,
   Unscrupulously bare,
The fatal splendour and beauty to our gaze
   Of Nature's dowry rare.

Around the leg a stocking rose-and-gold,
   Like a memento, stays;
The garter, like a vigilant eye, is roll'd
   And darts a diamond gaze.

The strange appearance of this solitude,
   The portrait there above,
Langorous, yet fierce in eyes and attitude,
   Tells of a gloomy love,

A guilty joy, and feasts with fiendish din
   And hellish kisses mad,
Whereat the swarm of evil spirits within
   The curtain's folds were glad.

And yet to note the graceful slenderness
   Of the marr'd shoulder's make,
The pointed hip, the figure's suppleness,
   As of a startled snake,

A MARTYR.

She is still so young! Her senses tired and slack
    And her exasperate soul,
Were they half-uncover'd to the thirsty pack
    Of lost desires and foul?

The vengeful man of whom a love so fresh
    Quench'd not the raging fire,
Fulfill'd he on the yielding, moveless flesh
    His boundless, fierce desire?

Answer, foul corpse! raised by thy tresses stiff
    With feverous arm, O tell,
Say, dreadful head, upon thy cold teeth if
    He seal'd the last farewell?

—Far from the mocking world, the crowd obscene,
    The gaping justice-room,
O sleep in peace, strange creature, sleep serene
    In thy mysterious tomb;

Thy husband roams the world: thy form divine
    Keeps vigil o'er his sleep;
His constancy will be as firm as thine
    To him, his faith as deep.

www.ingramcontent.com/pod-product-compliance
Lightning Source LLC
Chambersburg PA
CBHW020135170426
43199CB00010B/755